This book belongs to

Name *Esther Cantley*

Address _____

Date _____

A Look at the Church of God

A Look at the Church of God:

the story of the church
for children

1880-1930

by Merle D. Strege

Published by
Warner Press, Inc.
Anderson, Indiana

Copyright ©1987 by Warner Press, Inc.
ISBN 0-87162-481-8
All Rights Reserved
Printed in the United States of America
Warner Press, Inc.
Arlo F. Newell, Editor in Chief

Contents

To the Children

This book is written just for YOU! The Kid's Place Committee has dreamed of a way to share with you the heritage (story) of our church family known as the Church of God. That dream has come true with the publishing of this book.

Many of our ancestors—parents, grandparents, and great-grandparents—obeyed the biblical teaching in Deuteronomy 32:7 (NEB): "Remember the days of old, think of the generations of long ago; ask your father to recount it and your elders to tell you the tale." Have you heard this verse before? Thousands of persons have shared the story of our church through the years so that you may hear it today.

As you read this book, you will discover how the Church of God was started and how it grew. You will learn about different kinds of people who are part of the church family. We hope that you will be happy about being a special part of the Church of God family.

You belong to a large circle of friends who are learning about the Church of God. Remember what you are learning. Share this story with your friends. Someday, when you grow up, you may become one of the "ancestors" who will share the story of the church with others. Your sharing will keep the church family alive and growing. You will help the circle of friends to grow larger.

Enjoy your reading of this story. Celebrate your special place in God's family. Know that you are loved by God and the church family. Be glad as the story of the Church of God becomes YOUR story. We love you:

Lynn Ridenhour, Kid's Place Coordinator
and the Kid's Place Committee: Dan
Drummond, Deanna Edwards, Jacquie Gross,
Jeff Hayes, Diane Lindsey and Fran Strege

Preface

For more than one hundred years men and women, boys and girls, have been worshiping God in a group known as the Church of God. Their story has been told before, but this story is written just for children. From pictures and words printed in this book you can learn some important things about the first fifty years of the Church of God.

In the fifty years from 1880 to 1930 the message of the Church of God spread across the United States and Canada. From there missionaries carried the news to Mexico, Europe, Asia, and Africa. Missionary homes could be found in most of the great cities of the United States. Church of God people began orphanages and homes for the elderly. They founded training schools that grew into colleges. At the center of all this activity and energy was a magazine called the *Gospel Trumpet* published by dedicated women and men of the church. Spreading out from the Trumpet home, the message of the Church of God reached around the world at breathtaking speed.

In this book you will read about some of the events and the men and women of the first fifty years of the Church of God. You will see many pictures of places, people, and the kinds of things they did in those early years. We owe these people a great deal, for they laid the foundations of the Church of God in which we worship today.

Acknowledgements

Writing a book usually involves several people besides the author. This one is no exception, and I wish to thank those people who have had parts to play in its publication. Credit for the idea of a children's history of the Church of God must go to the Kid's Place Committee and especially Lynn Ridenhour and Fran Strege. Both of them also spent many hours searching for some of the photographs published here. Thanks must go to the Archives of the Church of God and the Editorial Division of Warner Press for opening their files to my use.

Joyce Krepshaw, faculty secretary at Anderson School of Theology, and Amy Biggerstaff, student typist, struggled with my bad writing in order to make the typescript.

Caroline Smith, of the Editorial Division at Warner Press, got the difficult assignment of making a pile of photographs and typed pages into a book that people could understand and use. She had very little time to accomplish that and has performed her task wonderfully.

All of these people have generously offered me all the help they could give. I'm sure that this small book could have been better, but any shortcomings in it are mine rather than theirs.

Merle D. Strege
Anderson, Indiana
Camp Meeting 1987

Chapter 1:
Beginnings

On October 1, 1881, a group of about thirty people met together in a church in the little village of Beaver Dam, Indiana. The village sat on the shore of Yellow Creek Lake in Kosciusko County in the northern part of the state. One of the people, a man named Daniel S. Warner, rose to his feet to speak to the group.

At that time Daniel Warner was the pastor of a church in Indianapolis and editor of a religious newspaper called the *Gospel Trumpet.* Earlier in his life he had been a soldier in the Civil War. Then in 1865 he decided to become a Christian and follow the Lord Jesus Christ. Soon after that he became a minister. He was a pastor in Ohio and Indiana, and he worked as a home missionary in Nebraska in the 1870s when that state was still part of the "Wild West."

All eyes in the room turned to Warner as he asked for permission to speak. His exact words were not written down, but we know that his speech attacked a problem in the lives of Christians in America. D.S. Warner saw

that the problem was that Christians had divided into too many different church groups. "Why should there be so many different churches?" he asked himself and the people around him. "Why must we divide ourselves into Baptists, Methodists, Lutherans, and all the others? Why can we not live together as brothers and sisters in one great church family under God?"

Warner believed that it was possible for Christians to live together in the unity that comes when God's love is present in people's

The Warner evangelistic company. These five people traveled together as flying messengers. Seated are D.S. Warner, the first editor of the Gospel Trumpet, and "Mother" Sarah Smith. Standing next to Warner, Barney E. Warren had to get permission from his parents to join Warner's company. Warren was a fine singer and songwriter. Many of his gospel songs are still sung in Church of God congregations. Next to him are Nanny Kigar and Frances Miller.

Early Church of God leaders included the two men in the front row. On the left, E. E. Byrum became the second editor of the Gospel Trumpet when D.S. Warner died in 1895. Standing next to him is Herbert McLellan Riggle, a famous preacher and author of several books.

hearts. At the Beaver Dam meeting he stood up to say that he was forever finished with all religious groups that divided Christian people from each other. From then on, he said, he would be part of God's church (or, the Church of God) and no other.

A group of Church of God ministers around 1900.

Mr. and Mrs. A. B. Palmer, early leaders in Michigan.

Rev. and Mrs. D.O. Teasley and Mr. Teasley's father. D.O. Teasley superintended the New York Missionary Home. He wrote books on how to plan a Sunday school and how to study the Bible. He also was a musician and songwriter. Some of his songs are in the Hymnal of the Church of God.

Warner asked the group if any others felt the way he did. Five people said they agreed with him. Two weeks later, in Carson City, Michigan, Warner made much the same speech. He had been invited there by Joseph and Allie Fisher, who agreed with him. Out of these two meetings, one in Indiana and the other in Michigan, the Church of God movement was born.

Early Church of God people were very determined not to be organized like the churches of their day. So they did not have church buildings and congregations as we do today. Instead they often met outdoors in what were called "brush arbors" when

At left, E.E. Byrum sits in a special room in the old Gospel Trumpet building. The room was dedicated to Byrum's ministry of divine healing. He believed very strongly in God's power to heal those who were sick. Hanging on the back wall are crutches, leg braces, bottles of medicine, and a hypodermic needle. These were given to Byrum by people who had been healed and no longer needed them. He thought of them as trophies that demonstrated the power of God. On the other walls there hung plaques and mottoes of the kind produced by the Gospel Trumpet Company. This prayer room became a famous place in the Church of God movement.

the weather permitted them to be outside.

In these early days they had neither church buildings nor pastors, as we think of them. Early Church of God ministers wanted to spread their message of the unity of God's people as fast and as far as possible. Because of their desire they were called the "Flying Messengers." They often traveled, either by train or wagon, in "evangelistic companies" made up of four or five men and women.

A company would travel into a town, sing a few songs, and announce that they would be holding a series of religious services (often called a "meeting"). At these services they would preach the message of the Church of God movement and they would sing songs written by men and women of the movement who put the message into poetry and music. Then the company would invite people in the audience to "take a stand" for the Church of God movement. At the end of the meeting, which might last as long as two weeks or a month, the evangelistic company would leave town and travel on to the

next place they felt God wanted them to have a meeting. These were great days in the Church of God, because the flying messengers and the *Gospel Trumpet* enabled the young movement to spread the word very fast. Before long little groups were meeting from coast to coast.

Black People and the Church of God

The Civil War was fought from 1860-1865 to end the slavery of black people in the southern states. During the war President Abraham Lincoln issued the Emancipation Proclamation, which declared that all slaves were free. In spite of these events black people continued to be treated unjustly by white people, especially after 1875, just about the time when the Church of God movement came into being.

Flying messengers like Lena Shoffner preached the message of Christian unity in the southern states just as they had everywhere else. Black people were especially interested in this message, because they believed that if Christians really followed that teaching, then blacks and whites would be able to

worship together in the same church.

In 1897 at the Alabama Camp Meeting, Miss Shoffner preached on the Bible verse that says "Christ has broken down the dividing wall of hostility." As she preached someone let loose a rope that separated the black and white sides of the congregation. Then all the worshipers, blacks and whites together, gathered at the altar to pray as brothers and sisters in the Lord. Some of the neighbors in the surrounding area became angry when they learned that blacks and whites worshiped together at the Church of God Camp Meeting. They threw rocks and tried to disrupt the meetings. They even dynamited some of the Camp Meeting buildings. But the saints held fast their

F.G. Smith was the third editor of the Gospel Trumpet from 1917 to 1930. In addition to editing, Smith also was a very influential author and preacher.

J.R. and Mabel Hale and their daughter Cleora. Before the Hales were married J.R. worked in the Gospel Trumpet office and Mabel (Asbenfelter) was an evangelist and pastor. She and Lena Shoffner were pastors of the First Church of God in Oklahoma City.

stand on Christian unity.

More than ten years before these exciting events a black woman named Jane Williams led a small gathering of black men and women in the Church of God way in Charleston, South Carolina. There were also congregations of black people in Augusta, Georgia in the 1890s.

After 1900 black Americans began moving to the great cities of the north—places like Chicago, Detroit, Philadelphia, and New York. Church of God black people were part of this move to the north and began worshiping with white people in the north. But congregations made up of only black people were begun in Chicago in 1915 and Detroit in 1916. By 1926 there were 62 black congregations and 2,276

Elsie Egermeier in 1916. Her Bible Storybook *is the best-selling book written by a Church of God author and published by the Gospel Trumpet Company.*

R.J. Smith pastored in Georgia, New York, and Pennsylvania. First president of the National Association of the Church of God, which began in 1917. The first camp meeting of black people in the Church of God met at West Middlesex, Pennsylvania, the same year.

members. At about the same time the National Association of the Church of God came into being. Since 1917 it has sponsored a Camp Meeting at West Middlesex, Pennsylvania. Large numbers of black Christians attend this meeting every year.

Pictured are the J.D. Smoots. J.D. Smoot was a popular preacher at Anderson Camp Meeting. He was a pastor evangelist in Missouri, Alabama, Pennsylvania, and Michigan. Smoot became a member of the Missionary Board of the Church of God in 1924.

S.P. Dunn entered the ministry in 1907. He was pastor for many years at Langley Avenue Church of God in Chicago. Dunn was a long-time member of the Board of Church Extension and Home Missions. He was also a trustee of Anderson College. Dunn Hall, on the college campus, is named in his honor.

Chapter 2: The Trumpet Family

Before the Church of God movement began, D.S. Warner already was writing and publishing the newspaper called the *Gospel Trumpet*. Along with a man named Haines, Warner began publishing the paper in January of 1881. In the early years of its life the paper was small, with only a few readers. For a while D.S. Warner wrote all the articles, set them in type for the printing press, and printed them on a hand press set up in the kitchen of the house where he and Mrs. Warner lived. When each issue of the paper was finished, he would take them out on the streets of Indianapolis and hand them out to passers-by on the street.

In the first thirty years that the *Gospel Trumpet* was published it moved its location several times. At one or another time it was located in Indianapolis; Rome City, Indiana; Cardington, Ohio; Bucyrus, Ohio; Williamston, Michigan; Grand Junction, Michigan; Moundsville, West Virginia; and Anderson, Indiana. Since 1906 the Church of God publishing company has

been in Anderson. Today it is called Warner Press, Inc.

Through the years the company grew. Three horse-drawn wagons carried all the equipment and supplies when the company moved to Bucyrus. In 1898 the company moved to Moundsville and that time they needed a special train to move all the equipment and people who were part of the company—nine freight cars, two passenger cars, and a baggage car.

The Gospel Trumpet Company, as it came to be known, did not hire people for an hourly wage, as companies do today. Until 1917 the newspaper, along with other products such as books, hymnals, almanacs, calendars, and wall plaques, was produced by a group of women and men known as the Trumpet family.

Above, *the bookstore of the Gospel Trumpet Company at Moundsville, West Virginia (1898-1906).*

Trumpet family members worked at all phases of the work of publishing. In the middle photo Barney Warren and others are composing songs that would appear in a songbook titled Truth in Song. *In the photo at the lower edge Gloria Campbell Heald operates a linotype machine. This machine placed together the heavy metal type pieces that were then set for printing.*

People joined the Trumpet family not to get a job for which they would be paid money, but because they believed in the message that was being published in the pages of the *Gospel Trumpet.* These people, many of them quite young, wanted to help spread the message of God's love that brings Christian unity.

Because workers did not receive pay for their labor they all lived together as a large family. They ate their meals together, worshiped together, went on outings, studied, and prayed together. They slept in quarters provided by the company. Often these were large dormitory-like buildings, called Trumpet Homes.

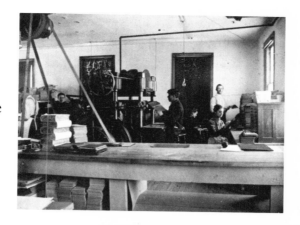

Other parts of Trumpet operations were office, shipping, and subscriptions. Orders had to be processed and then the products had to be shipped. Below, some of the Trumpet workers are trying out the first truck owned by the company. Before it was purchased in 1907, shipments and deliveries were made by horse-drawn wagon.

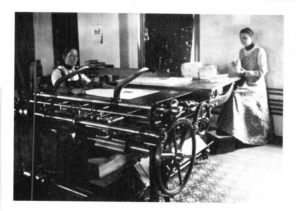

The Trumpet family almost always did their own work, so that, for example, when they moved to Anderson in 1906 some of the family workers spent all their time making heavy concrete blocks that were used to construct the publishing plant, the Trumpet home, an Old People's home, and several other buildings.

When a Trumpet worker's clothing wore out he or she would go to the home manager or matron who would get replacement clothing from a common storehouse. Some clothing was donated to the

The Gospel Trumpet Company building in Moundsville, West Virginia.

The Trumpet home in Anderson, Indiana. All workers lived together here until 1917.

All aspects of life were shared by Trumpet family members. Above, they are seen eating together. Pictured at the right is Mother O'Brien. She was a Trumpet worker at Moundsville. Unlike some of the other workers, she did not run a press or operate a linotype machine. Mother O'Brien did not write any books or compose any songs. She was the laundress who saw to it that other Trumpet workers had clean clothes so that they could be free to write and operate the publishing equipment.

company. But members of
the family also were
assigned the task of making
clothes.

In 1888 the Trumpet
family numbered only six
people. But as the
publishing work grew, so
did the number of family
members. Feeding and
clothing so many people
meant that some Trumpet
family members worked at
jobs that had nothing to do
with printing, but were
absolutely necessary for the
support of the people who
did the printing work.
When Otto F. Linn came to
work for the Gospel
Trumpet Company his first
job was taking care of
chickens. At breakfast
Trumpet family members
were nourished on the eggs
laid by Otto's chickens.
Other Trumpet family
members worked in
vegetable gardens and
orchards, tended pigs,
milked cows, washed and
ironed clothes, or even
tended the Trumpet family
cemetery. Everyone in the
family shared in the work
of one another.

By 1917, however, the
Trumpet family had grown
large and experienced many
problems. For example,
some of the family
members in the Trumpet

home in Anderson complained that others were too noisy. The family system was dropped. Since then the people who worked at Gospel Trumpet Company, and now Warner Press, are paid wages for their labor. After 1917 the company did not attempt to provide food, clothing, and shelter for all of the people who worked at spreading the news of the Church of God movement.

Members of the Trumpet family at work in the sewing room. These people made clothes for the common storeroom. When a Trumpet family member needed a new piece of clothing, he or she went to the storeroom and got the necessary item. Clothing was furnished at no cost to workers because they did not receive salaries. Below, a group of workers relax in the evening in the Trumpet home lounge.

Providing for Trumpet family members meant doing lots of jobs that were not related to printing. In winter, blocks of ice had to be cut out of lakes and rivers to be stored in ice houses so that people could keep perishable goods in iceboxes in warm weather. Coal had to be purchased and carried to large bins in the building basements. Coal heated buildings and drove the steam engines that powered Trumpet machinery. Pigs had to be tended before they were turned into ham, bacon, and pork chops for hungry Trumpet workers. The Trumpet company had its own fire department and even its own band.

Chapter 3: Gatherings

Every year, during the third week of June, thousands of people, many of them from beyond the borders of the United States, travel to Anderson, Indiana. They come to attend the International Convention of the Church of God, better known as Anderson Camp Meeting.

Throughout the summer months state and district camp meetings also take place. More than eighty such camp meetings were held in 1980. But the largest of Church of God camp meetings is the one that meets in Anderson. Why call it camp meeting? And why does it meet in Anderson?

Camp meetings have been part of American religious life since the very early 1800s. Settlers in Tennessee and on both sides of the Ohio River in Kentucky, Ohio, and Indiana joined together in the first camp meetings. Those were rough days on the frontier of the Old Northwest. People were glad to be together with other settlers. They were willing to live in rough circumstances in order to enjoy each other's

Annual National
CAMP MEETING
OF THE CHURCH OF GOD
ANDERSON, INDIANA
JUNE 13-22, 1919

Evangelists From All Parts of the Country Will Be in Attendance

This great assembly will be a source of spiritual profit to you, as it has been to thousands of others who have attended in former years from all over the world. There will be discourses on

The Unity of God's People,   Divine Healing of the Body,
Salvation From Sin,   Fulfilment of Prophecy,
Purity of Heart and Life, and other subjects of interest in the religious world today.

DAILY SERVICES
10:30 a. m., 2:15 p. m. and 8:00 p. m.

Besides these there will be services for children and for young people, also divine healing and baptismal services. Assistant Surgeon W. F. King, of the U. S. Public Health Service, will address the Assembly at 2:15 P. M., June 17, in the interests of the campaign against venereal disease.

Lunches and refreshments can be procured on the grounds. Lodging, $2.00 for entire meeting or 40c by the single night. One fourth discount if bedding is brought. Tents and special lodging at various prices.

A Large Tabernacle, Capable of Seating 5,000 Persons, was Completed Last Year

---

Camp ground adjoins the Gospel Trumpet Company's publishing plant, just east of the city limits, and is on the Muncie Division of the Union Traction Co. of Ind. Interurban cars stop at grounds.

There will be opportunity to be shown through the large up-to-date publishing office.

COME AND HEAR THE GOSPEL IN SERMON AND IN GOOD SPIRITUAL SINGING

S.L. and Amanda Speck with their family at one of the early general camp meetings, probably at Moundsville.

The campground during Grand Junction, Michigan, camp meeting.

fellowship. The first few camp meetings just sort of happened, without much planning. In a few years they became such a success that church people organized them and camp meetings became a regular feature of frontier American life. So, when the first general Church of God camp meeting was announced for Bangor, Michigan, June 10-20, 1886, there was nothing new about the idea of gathering for religious meetings.

Church of God people gave different names to the various sorts of meetings they held. Camp meetings occurred in the summer and campers always used tents. Grove meetings also took place in the summer, but no tents were used. People were concerned that the meetings be correctly named. You can imagine how upset you would be if you went to a meeting where you thought tents would be provided and then learned after you got there that you'd be sleeping under the stars. What if it rained?!

Southerners often used the term *brush arbor meetings* to label their annual meetings. Winter weather did not stop Church of God people from joining for good singing and preaching. But in winter they changed the name to assembly meetings, which were held indoors—except for baptisms, which sometimes meant that holes were cut in the ice-covered rivers and lakes so that new Christians could be baptized.

The general camp meeting convenes in Anderson every year because since 1906 Anderson has been the location of the publishing company of the Church of God. From 1896 to 1906 the general camp meeting was at Moundsville, West Virginia, the site of the Gospel Trumpet Company during those years.

The publishing company was the center of life and activity in the early Church of God movement, much like the hub of a bicycle wheel. Messages about revivals, evangelistic work,

Baptism has always been important to Church of God people. On the campground at Anderson they built a permanent baptismal pool, shown below. Baptisms might occur at any meetings and in any season. In January 1909 holes were cut in ice-covered Lake Michigan so that new Christians could be baptized, as shown above.

Large crowds of people have attended camp meeting in Anderson. Their needs had to be met for the week they came to the meeting. Those needs might be finding a parking place for their cars or being fed. Below are pictured the people who worked in the dining hall at the 1912 Anderson Camp Meeting.

Many camp meeting services took place in tents. But in Anderson, Church of God people built a large tabernacle for the general worship services. Above is a photo taken at 1918 Anderson Camp Meeting. Notice the signs with Bible verse messages painted on them.

or where ministers were going next, were mailed in to the Trumpet office. Some of these were printed in a section called "News from the Field." In this way Church of God people could keep track of each other as information came in and went out of the Trumpet office. Some rooms in the Trumpet home also were used as a kind of hotel for weary flying messengers and gospel workers. Once rested they would return to their evangelistic work. For these reasons the location of the publishing company has tended to be the natural gathering place of Church of God people. So it seemed logical for the general camp meeting to meet in the same place.

Chapter 4:
Missionary Homes

Many people in the Church of God movement liked the way the Trumpet workers lived and worked together. So the Trumpet home became a model for the life together of ministers and gospel workers in other places in the United States. At one time or another some forty-five of these missionary homes existed from New York to San Diego and from Grand Forks, North Dakota to El Paso, Texas.

The first of the missionary homes was built by Jacob and Jennie Byers about 1893 in San Diego, California. But in 1906 they moved to Oakland to begin a new missionary home.

The home in Chicago came to be among the largest and most extensive of the Church of God missionary homes. Gorham Tufts founded it in 1895. For the first eight or nine years the Chicago home focused its attention on caring for jobless and homeless men by providing housing and meals. Tufts also worked hard preaching the good news of Christ's love to these victims of society.

Later the leaders of the Chicago home put more emphasis on evangelism, teaching, providing accommodations for traveling ministers, and distributing the literature of the Gospel Trumpet Company. Thus the home became an important part of the spreading message of the *Gospel Trumpet* and the Church of God movement.

Church of God people were very creative in thinking of ways to share

George T. Clayton, pictured left with his wife, built a church boat that navigated the Ohio River from 1894 to 1898. The boat was named the Floating Bethel. Clayton not only built the boat but he directed the worship services on board. The Floating Bethel was used to carry the message of the Church of God to Ohio river towns. Clayton had planned to let his vessel float down the Ohio to the Mississippi and then on the Gulf of Mexico. But a fire destroyed the Floating Bethel while it was docked at Moundsville.

the message of salvation and the unity of all Christians. The message was told in the paper, the *Gospel Trumpet*, in books written by Church of God writers, in the songs they wrote and sang, and in small booklets and pamphlets called tracts.

Some of this material was given away at no cost; anyone who could not afford to subscribe to the *Gospel Trumpet* could have it free for the asking. Copies often were given to inmates in prisons. Church of God people frequently left copies of the *Trumpet* in public places, such as park benches or in train stations, anywhere a passerby might be likely to pick up a newspaper and begin reading. Sometimes the Gospel Trumpet Company would mail a bundle of the

People in the Church of God have been concerned to help people not as fortunate as themselves. Sebastian Michels founded the Old Peoples' Home in South Haven, Michigan. Homes for the elderly also were built in Anderson and St. Paul Park, Minnesota. The Gospel Trumpet Company also published books and papers in braille for the blind. Grace Defore, in the center of the photo below, began a publishing work for the blind in Pomona, California. She joined the Trumpet family after it moved to Anderson in 1906.

papers to a town, in care of its postmaster, with instructions to place as many as he or she could in the mailboxes of the townspeople.

An important way that the message of the Church of God spread was through the efforts of men and women called *colporteurs*. These people felt a special responsibility to distribute books, tracts, and the *Gospel Trumpet*. They were almost like traveling salespersons, sometimes journeying far and wide to sell the literature of the Church of God movement. When they sold out their supplies they would often return to one of the missionary homes for a short rest. Soon, with their supplies replenished, off they would go again.

Another activity in the

Above, *George and Mary Cole, superintendents of the Chicago Missionary Home.*

Pictured here are three of the missionary homes that operated between 1895 and the early 1920s. Upper left is the New York home. Middle left is the home in St. Louis, Missouri. The picture below shows the missionary home in St. Joseph, Michigan. This home's staff used two languages, English and German, since many German-speaking immigrants lived in the surrounding area.

missionary homes was teaching. New converts to the movement learned biblical truths in "cottage prayer meetings" led by missionary home workers. Young men and women whom God had called to ministry received training and instruction in ministerial study courses offered in some of the missionary homes.

As in the Trumpet homes, not all the missionary home workers were involved in religious work. Some did the "spiritual" work of evangelism, colporteuring, and teaching; others did the cooking, housekeeping, and building maintenance.

For about twenty-five

The Church of God has done missionary work among many different ethnic groups in the United States. J. Frank Shaw, upper right, began missionary work among native Americans in the Tulalip Reservation in northwest Washington. Constantine Nicholas began Church of God work among Greek-speaking Americans in 1916. Among the many young Greek converts to the Church of God was Nick Zazanis, pictured right, along with his family. Zazanis became pastor of a Greek congregation in Chicago in 1922. There he also began editing the Gospel Trumpet in Greek. The congregation is pictured lower right, gathered for an outing on Independence Day, 1926.

years the missionary homes of the Church of God filled an important role in the movement's ministry to the cities of America and in the training of young people who wanted to serve God and the church in ministry. About 1920 the missionary homes began closing as the services they provided were taken over by other boards and agencies of the movement. But they remain a colorful and important part of the heritage of the Church of God movement.

Church of God people worked among many immigrant people. Andreas and Anastasia Kandler began a church in the early 1900s in St. Paul, Minnesota for Hungarian- and German-speaking people. They translated Church of God songs into Hungarian so they could be sung by the newcomers. The other photo shows the interior of Langeson Chapel in Hutchinson, Minnesota. Some of the mottoes on the walls are printed in the Norwegian language. For about twenty years the Church of God published books, pamphlets, mottoes in Norwegian and Swedish for Scandinavian immigrants. In Norwegian, the Gospel Trumpet was called Den Evageliske Basan.

Chapter 5: The Church of God in Foreign Lands

I n 1891 a man named B.F. Elliot decided that God wanted him to go to Mexico. At the time Elliot lived in Santa Barbara, California. Often on street corners he preached the message of the Church of God movement. When Elliot decided he would become a missionary to Mexico he realized he would need to be able to speak to the Mexicans in their own language. He borrowed a Spanish grammar book and a Spanish New Testament and then taught himself the language.

Accompanied by his five-year-old son and a man named S.C. Shaw, Elliot sailed from San Diego to Ensenada in the area of Mexico called Baja, California. Elliot and Shaw went from one door to the next, telling people of God's love for them and that their sins could be forgiven. A man who supported them in their work loaned them his donkey, and so they journeyed south distributing Spanish New Testaments and sharing the gospel of Jesus Christ.

B.F. Elliot established a

permanent mission in Ensenada. He traveled through western Mexico on four missionary journeys between 1891 and 1899. His efforts mark what is considered to be the first genuine missionary work by people of the Church of God.

Missionary work in the Church of God was greatly strengthened through the life and ministry of A.D. Khan. He grew up in East Bengal, India, in a strict Muslim family.

In 1893 he became a Christian and this greatly upset his parents. They tried everything they could imagine to win him back to their religion—magical charms, long arguments, even prison! Nothing worked, and so they cast him out of their family.

Khan studied at the

Pictured are Georgia C. and B.F. Elliot, the first Church of God missionaries to Mexico. Below left is George P. Tasker, who, along with his wife, went as missionaries to India in the early 1900's. There he became close friends with A. D. Khan (right). Khan had begun the Church of God's work in India after corresponding with E.E. Byrum. Together Khan and Tasker were the leading figures of the Church of God mission in India.

The missions group during the 1919-1920 school year at Anderson Bible Training School.

London Mission College in Calcutta. Through his study there he began to question the customary practice of dividing Christianity into different denominations. About the same time he heard of the Church of God movement in the United States. Khan wrote to E.E. Byrum, who became the editor of the *Gospel Trumpet* in 1896, for more information. Early in 1897 the company shipped a thousand pounds of books and tracts to Khan. They also sent him two handpresses, which he put to use publishing a paper called *The Firebrand*. Church of God people in the United States also sent money to India so that people could buy food in the years of great famine that were then ravaging India.

In 1903 Byrum invited Khan to visit the United States. Khan's tour of America and visits to many Church of God

Church of God missionaries were active in Europe beginning in the 1890s. Pictured here are Jens P. N. Ikast and his family, missionaries to Denmark. Below is a photo of the "Gospel Van," used for meetings in Birkenhead, England in 1894. Seated in the van are Lena Sholfner, Hattie Rupert and J. H. Rupert.

congregations sparked great enthusiasm for the missionary cause. His book *India's Millions*, written while he was traveling in America, inspired many Church of God men and women to consider going into missionary service.

The blossoming work in India received a great deal of attention and support from America. Along with Khan other Indian church leaders were R.N. Mundul, Mosir Moses, and J.J.M. Roy. They built a prospering work in several different regions of the country. The church in America began sending missionaries to India in 1904. By 1910 eleven missionaries were serving there. In these early years the work in India was the largest missionary venture of the Church of God movement.

Asia was an important early Church of God mission field. Pictured here, from top to bottom are J. J. and Evalyn Nichols-Roy (India), Mr. and Mrs. William Hunnex (China), Mr. and Mrs. A. U. Yajima (Japan), and mission workers at the mission in Lahore, India.

From 1900 to 1925 missionaries of the Church of God went from North America to China, Japan, Africa, the Middle East, and other places around the world. Their stories are great adventures of courage, hardship, and faith. Tens of thousands of people have been blessed through the dedicated service of these men and women.

Chapter 6: Schools

A seminary is a special kind of school where people study in order to become better prepared for being a minister. The Church of God has had a seminary in Anderson since 1950. But where did men and women in the Church of God learn how to be ministers before there was a seminary?

Preparing young men and women for gospel work was important to early Church of God leaders. But in the movement's first years people did not attend schools for that preparation. In the very early years a young man or woman learned how to be a minister through on-the-job training. Sometimes a more experienced minister would offer advice, but other times young ministers learned through trial and error how to care for people.

Early Church of God leaders were deeply suspicious of colleges and seminaries. They thought that education could not substitute for God's call to the ministry. So they called colleges and seminaries "preacher factories." By this they meant that they disapproved of such places.

But because the early leaders disapproved of colleges and seminaries does not mean that they did not think training for ministers was important.

Before he died in 1895, D.S. Warner was making plans for a ministers' training institute at the Trumpet workers' home in Grand Junction, Michigan. His plans were dropped when he died. Other young people learned about the ministry at some of the missionary homes. The homes in Spokane, Kansas City, and especially New York City wanted to provide study courses for ministerial students. The New York City home

Above, J.T. Wilson and family. Wilson, general manager of the Gospel Trumpet Company, served as principal of Anderson Bible Training School when its doors first opened for classes in 1917. Wilson was the person who originally had the idea to start a school for ministers at Anderson.

John A. Morrison was pastoring a church in Delta, Colorado, when J.T. Wilson asked him to come to Anderson in 1919. Wilson wanted Morrison to become the new principal of the Bible training school. Morrison accepted the invitation and became the first president of Anderson College, as the training school later was renamed. Morrison led the school for thirty-nine years.

developed a home study course for people who lived far away from New York. It is important to remember that these early ministerial training courses were about the only form of schools that the Church of God had prior to 1917.

About this same time a man named J.T. Wilson got the idea to begin a regular school for ministerial students. The school would have regular teachers that would hold classes. Wilson was the general manager of the Gospel Trumpet Company and they became the sponsor of the school when it opened for classes in 1917. That year the

The training school's graduating class of 1920. In those days graduates did not receive diplomas. The school gave out Ministers Certificates instead.

Amy Lopez was a professor of English at Anderson College. Born in Jamaica, she came to the United States in 1923. She also was Dean of Women at Anderson College.

Russell L. Olt, first dean of Anderson College. He served in this job for thirty-three years. Olt came to the college at the request of President Morrison. Olt moved to Anderson from Wilmington, Ohio. For some years he pastored a church there on weekends while working during the week as dean of the college. He was a strong supporter of the rights of working people and worked very hard on behalf of refugees and the homeless.

Trumpet family disbanded and moved out of the company-owned home. Anderson Bible Training School moved into the vacant building and the first classes were taught on October 2. Only a handful of students attended and, like the teachers, nearly all of them were full-time workers at the Gospel Trumpet Company; they attended school on their own time.

J.T. Wilson was followed as principal of the school by John A. Morrison. He guided the fragile institution through some very hard times. But still it grew. By 1929, after Morrison had been president for ten years, the school's name became Anderson College and Theological Seminary. It began offering courses of study to students who wanted to become teachers or social workers as well as

In the first years of operation the whole school was housed in the building shown above. The Bible training school took over the Trumpet home in 1917 from the Gospel Trumpet Company. Students ate, slept, and went to class, all in this one building, which became known as "Old Main." Below, a group of students are pictured eating in the school cafeteria.

courses for ministers. Later it became an accredited liberal arts college.

Anderson College is the oldest and largest of the Church of God colleges. It is by no means the only one. J.T. Wilson started another school named Warner Memorial University, but it lasted only a short while. People in the Pacific Northwest founded Pacific Bible Institute before 1920, but it ended in the 1920s. In 1937 Pacific Bible College was founded in Spokane, Washington. Later it became Warner Pacific College. Other colleges begun after 1930 include Mid-America Bible College, Bay Ridge Christian College, Warner Southern College, and in Canada, Gardner Bible College. Another college with some connection to the Church of God is Azusa Pacific University in California.

Pictured here are the faculty and students of the school in one of its first years of operation.

ANDERSON (INDIANA) COLLEGE LADIES QUARTET

Mrs. Virgil Johnson, Second Soprano   Miss Opal Davis, First Alto

Mrs. John Lackey, First Soprano   Miss Eva Clare Holbrook, Second Alto

Mr. John Lackey, Manager

Sebastian Michels heard the message of the Church of God movement in 1882. He believed in the movement's vision of holiness and unity so much that in 1883 he began preaching to others about the Church of God.

Michels had a tender spot in his heart for children. His concern for them led him to establish a children's home. The first home was in Grand Junction; later he built a second at South Haven, Michigan. Many "flying messengers" had families. The adults did not want their children to have to travel with the gospel workers. Michels's children's home became a place where flying messengers could leave their children safe and secure in the care of people they trusted. Later Michels expanded his home to include care for some orphans. In this way it became an orphanage.

Sebastian Michels's children's home and orphanage was an exception to early Church of God attitudes toward children. Leaders like D.S. Warner were very suspicious of the kind of children's work

Chapter 7:
Children and the Church of God

they saw in church denominations. So in the first decades of the Church of God, children did not attend Sunday schools because there were none. But Warner did believe that a great need existed for teaching children from the Bible itself.

Because other people shared Warner's idea, Sunday schools for children and teen-agers began to be established. As the number of Sunday schools increased people began to see that some group needed to encourage their further growth. In 1923 the General Ministerial Assembly created the Board of Religious Education and Sunday Schools. Today this group is called the Board of Christian Education.

Two people who were very important for the Christian education of children were Bessie L. Byrum and Elsie Egermeier. Bessie Byrum worked very hard as a member and president of the Sunday

Above and center *is Sebastian Michels's children's home in Grand Junction, Michigan. As many as sixty children at one time lived in Michels' orphanage.* Below *are the children's home staff and residents in 1895. Mr. and Mrs. Michels are seated together in the second row left. He is the man with the beard.*

School Board. Elsie Egermeier wrote a book that is among the all-time best-selling Church of God books—*Egermeier's Bible Storybook.* The stories of the Bible were retold in the Bible storybook in words that children could understand.

Early Church of God people often felt that the home was the best place for children to learn about God and the stories of the Bible. Elsie Egermeier had written her storybook to be used in home settings. Sometimes family houses substituted for church buildings. Often they were decorated with plaques and wall mottoes sold by the Gospel Trumpet Company. By using such decorations parents could create for their children a home atmosphere that emphasized Christianity.

Another part of life in many Church of God homes was house worship. Prayer, singing, and Bible reading were supposed to be a regular part of family life. Even children as young

The children of Trumpet worker William A. Bixler: Leon, Lola, Inez, Virginia, Lucille, and Thelma. Some early Church of God children lived in homes where family worship looked like the picture below.

as three years old were expected to listen to adults read and explain sections from the Bible.

Today some of us might think that Church of God people had very strict homes. But in many ways they were not very different from most American families around 1900. Parents were advised to "govern" their children and not let their children govern them. Children were expected to do exactly as their parents desired. Sometimes parents got their children to do as they wished by setting a good example. When good examples failed, parents tried other methods, such as punishment. Advice given to Church of God parents said they should not "cuff," "slap," or pull ears. But they could paddle, if they used a paddle that was the right size for the child—big paddles for older, larger kids; small paddles for the younger and small ones.

Church of God families

Some early Church of God children grew up in towns and cities, just like today. Shown above is a vacation church school parade in downtown Anderson, Indiana. Other Church of God children grew up in rural settings like those pictured.

sometimes had some different ideas about the kinds of food that were good for people to eat. Usually they preferred simple foods—vegetables, meat, fruit, and cereal. They did not eat many fancy desserts or sweets. Mostly they drank water or milk. When they wanted a hot beverage they drank a roasted grain drink called Postum.

Clothing also was very simple for most Church of God families. Women avoided skirts with lots of pleats and ruffles. Their blouses often had high necks and long sleeves. Men wore dark suits and, for a few years, refused to wear neckties. They believed the tie was a sign of worldly pride. Children wore clothing like that of their playmates at school and in the neighborhood.

Camp meeting organizers planned for children long before the days of Kids' Place. Above is a photo of the children's play area (called a park) at Grand Junction, Michigan, campground. Below, at another campground is a sandbox, reserved for kids only.